151 Affirmations for Creative People

Healing Words and How to Use Them

Dianna Gunn

For Sam, whose friendship has inspired me to do much more than write this book.

Contents

My Journey of Affirmation

The time is 11:30 at night. I save my video game—*Dragon Age: Inquisition*, this week—and switch to a familiar show, one of my regular roster of comfort shows. I retrieve my journal, a simple spiral-bound notebook, from its shelf. After recording my pain levels for the day, I move on to a more esoteric form of writing.

The exercise reminds me of an elementary school assignment, the "I am" poem. Most of the sentences even start with those same two words, "I am."

This time, though, I'm not writing about things I already am. At least, not things I already *believe* I am. I'm writing what I *want* to believe I am.

My sentences look something like this:

- I am strong, confident, and capable

- I am growing, learning, and changing all of the time

- I am powerful

These words stir up a complicated mix of feelings. Imposter syndrome, because I struggle to believe these things about myself. Hope, because I can see how my life would change if I truly held these beliefs in my soul. Excitement, because these sentences feel more real than they did before, and soon enough, I'll be able to replace them with other beliefs I need to work on.

This is my affirmation practice. It's a bright spot in my day and one of the most important parts of my routine. With it, I've grown from struggling to write "I like myself" to writing "I love myself" without a shadow of doubt.

I wasn't always a fan of affirmations, though. In fact, I took over a decade to warm up to the idea.

My childhood was marred by the stress of poverty and bullying. I often woke up with a "stomach ache" bad enough to keep me home from school, but those stomach aches almost always disappeared around lunchtime. I've since learned that this is one of the most common ways anxiety expresses itself in children, which makes sense: my mind has always been both my greatest ally and my worst enemy.

The pain intensified when my dad was diagnosed with cancer and eventually died. Retreating into stories was no longer enough; I turned to self-harm instead. I also contemplated suicide for the first time.

I knew this level of pain wasn't typical. Other people might struggle with grief and self-esteem issues, but they didn't want to make themselves bleed. They didn't have constant thoughts of suicide or a hundred poems contemplating what death was like.

I turned to the internet for answers. The internet was a different place back then, but there were already millions of people sharing their stories through forums, chatrooms, and blogs. The well of human suffering was endless, and while my feelings weren't *normal*, I wasn't alone either.

Some of the stories I found talked about people who reached the other side. People who had spent years in the agony of grief and self-hatred and had eventually, often through sheer force of will, pulled themselves out of it.

I became obsessed with these stories, and with the advice these people offered. But there was one thing I dismissed right away: the idea of affirmations. Frankly, I thought they sounded silly. I believed the only thing I would feel if I practiced affirmations was embarrassed. So I left them out of my journals.

Looking back on it, I can see this as a symptom of a larger problem. Back then, I wasn't interested in self-acceptance, let alone self-love. My only desire was to stop hurting, to pour my grief onto the page and be free of it so I could survive long enough to share my stories with the world.

Grief for someone like a parent is complex. We're never fully rid of it. Over time, however, my grief became manageable. I released most of it into journals, and I learned to carry what remained as a badge of honor, a reminder of love rather than of loss.

As my wounds closed, my focus shifted. I stopped journaling about the past and started journaling about the future. I became more regular in my journaling too, with an almost-daily practice built to combat my anxiety.

Then COVID-19 came along and derailed, well, everything except my journaling. I began pouring five, ten, sometimes even fifteen pages into my journal in every session.

In the midst of this, my best friend (hi, Sam!) asked if I used affirmations. This time, something about the suggestion clicked. Affirmations seemed not only useful but like the next logical evolution in my journaling practice.

Since then, I've developed a robust affirmation practice. They have a special place in my nightly journaling, between my to-do list and my gratitude entries. I created all of my own affirmations, writing what felt right and evolving those affirmations over time. This practice brings a sense of joy and calmness into my nightly routine and has, over time, begun to change the way I see myself.

For the first time in my life, I'm able to write "I love myself" without cringing. Most nights, I even believe it.

Now I want to pass this gift on to you. This book will show you how to develop an affirmation practice that fits your life, provide you with 151 affirmations to choose from, and help you create your own affirmations when the ones listed no longer work for you. With this knowledge, you'll be able to start changing your mind and, hopefully, your life.

How to Use This Book

What this book won't do

Before we dive into how to use this book, I want to make a few things clear. First, I'm not a therapist or a doctor of any kind. I haven't taken a psychology course beyond the high school level.

What you'll find in this book is my own personal process, developed without the oversight of a therapist or medical professional of any kind. This process is meant for use in combination with medical intervention, not as a replacement for it. I personally spent two years on antidepressant medication and without it, I wouldn't have reached the point of developing an affirmation practice in the first place.

Second, this book can't erase systemic oppression. Changing your mindset won't remove every barrier in your path if you're a marginalized person. It can, however, stop *you* from being a barrier to your own success.

About the affirmations in this book

As you read through this book, you'll notice that a lot of the affirmations are quite similar. This is because writing the same exact words every day eventually becomes routine. At first, this is great because the words are coming naturally. After a while, however, you start writing statements by rote. You're no longer present with the words, so they lose their power.

If this starts to happen before you've truly internalized the belief you're affirming, you'll need to evolve your affirmation without changing the meaning. Even a change of one or two words can make the affirmation feel new.

The other reason I've included variations for the most important affirmations is that words feel different to each person. The words I'm comfortable using might not feel right to you. This makes it important to include as many options as possible, in the hopes of providing value to a greater number of people.

My affirmation practice

With those disclaimers in mind, let's dive into my personal process.

The first thing I want to stress is that I don't pressure myself to journal every night. In fact, I deliberately take Saturday nights off. If life gets in the way, or even if I get sucked into a TV show and go straight from binge-watching to bed, I forgive myself. We live in a world where every hobby is expected to be monetized, every moment optimized. Putting that same pressure on our journaling practice is a great way to make ourselves hate journaling.

On the other hand, letting the habit lapse for more than a couple of days leads to a steady deterioration of my mental health. So I aim for 3-5 journaling sessions per week. In each journaling session, I write out at least five affirmations. On Sundays, and any night when I have the energy, I'll write out a full page of affirmations.

Every couple of months, I sit down to journal *about* my affirmations. I consider how each one makes me feel, and if needed, I make a change. I do this partially to keep the affirmations fresh; my mind gets bored when a routine becomes, well, too routine. The change also acknowledges the changes happening within me, because when you put daily work into yourself, growth never stops.

This book will walk you through the steps of building your own affirmation practice, based on the practice I have developed for myself.

151 Affirmations for Creative People: The Workbook

Want some more hands-on guidance for creating your affirmation practice? Check out *151 Affirmations for Creative People: The*

Workbook. This mini-workbook features questions designed to help you with every aspect of building your affirmation practice, from choosing your affirmations to creating new affirmations of your own.

151 Affirmations for Creative People: The Workbook is designed as a companion to the main *151 Affirmations for Creative People* book. You can buy it in paperback through Amazon or grab the PDF edition from https://ko-fi.com/diannagunn/shop.

How To Develop Your Own Affirmation Practice

Before you can create an effective affirmation practice, you'll need to reflect on your existing routines and preferences. This will help you shape a unique practice rooted in your reality, rather than forcing you to work with someone else's formula.

In the next couple of pages, I'll explore the things you need to consider as you plan your affirmation practice.

Spoken vs written affirmations

When I first encountered the idea of affirmations (I'll be honest, I don't remember what self-help book it was), the suggestion was to say them out loud. The idea was to harness the power of the spoken word, to make something real by externalizing it. You can amplify this further by saying your affirmations while looking in a mirror, meeting the eyes of your reflection to personally deliver yourself a message.

The logic behind this approach is sound. Words spoken, whether spoken out loud or signed, can feel more real than our thoughts. They become part of the outer world, rather than the inner world. For many people, spoken affirmations are the way to go.

On the other hand, there are several reasons why spoken affirmations might not work for you. Maybe you share a small space and you feel self-conscious about the idea of someone walking in on (or otherwise observing) you during your affirmation practice. Or you might have health issues that make it difficult or even impossible to speak or sign your affirmations on a regular basis. Or you might find that you just don't like the sensation of speaking your affirmations, whether through verbal speech or sign language. In these instances, written affirmations make more sense.

Written affirmations also have the advantage of creating a permanent record. If you write your affirmations, pretty soon you'll have a notebook full of positive statements about yourself. You can then turn to your notebook of affirmations any time you're looking for a mental boost. This record will also make it easier to evaluate and evolve your affirmations practice over time.

Both spoken and written affirmations have their advantages and disadvantages. The key is to find a way to make your affirmation practice comfortable enough to repeat it 3-5 times a week. You want the affirmations to be what challenges you, not the affirmations practice itself.

If you're not sure what type of affirmation you're most suited to, try them both! Sometimes the only way to find the best approach for you is to experiment.

Consistency without guilt

The power of affirmations lies in their ability to gradually replace negative self-talk with more positive ideas. To get the full effect, you need to find a place for affirmations in your daily routine.

This might seem contradictory; didn't I say that I don't do my affirmations every day just a couple of pages ago?

The truth is, I don't do *anything* other than eating, drinking, and sleeping every single day. Having one or two days per week where my only responsibility is taking care of my biological functions gives me space to recharge. I also live with multiple disabilities, and some days those biological functions are all I can manage.

Reality is complicated. At any given time, most of us are juggling jobs, side hustles, families, housework, and creative hobbies. The average person can't afford to pause these things to focus on personal development. We need to fit it around all of our other obligations. Sometimes, it simply won't make it into our day.

If we beat ourselves up about missing a day, we create a cycle of guilt and shame. The more days we miss, the more guilt we feel. We quickly come to associate the whole practice of affirmations with guilt and shame, which makes us want to do them even less.

The cycle is insidious, and it happens every time we tell ourselves we must do something every single day.

Where we make space, then, is in the routine we follow on an average day. Our most strict routines tend to exist shortly after we wake up and before we go to bed, making these ideal times for integrating new habits. Many people also already include journaling in their morning or evening routine, which can easily include affirmations.

The key to success here is to tie your affirmation practice to something you're already doing. This will help you make it just another part of your day.

You also want to start small, using 3-5 affirmations in your regular practice. Challenging long-held negative thought patterns is hard work. You're more likely to stick with it if you choose a few thoughts to challenge at a time. As you grow more comfortable with your practice, you can expand this; I often do a full page of affirmations.

How to choose your affirmations

There are 151 affirmations in this book. How are you supposed to narrow it down to the 3 – 5 affirmations you're supposed to start with?

In my experience, the most powerful affirmations share two characteristics:

- **They challenge thoughts you have on a regular basis.** For example, if you struggle to find the confidence to apply for paid creative opportunities, you might choose an affirmation like "I deserve to be paid for my art".

- **They focus on things you're working to develop.** Affirmations on their own have limited value. If you're not taking steps to make your affirmations real, they'll ring false. This can make the whole practice feel futile.

As you read the affirmations in this book, take a moment to sit with each one and how it feels to you. Do you believe this statement already? If not, what would change if you did believe this statement? How would you approach life differently with this belief?

If you find yourself growing excited, and maybe a little bit nervous, about these changes, you've landed on an affirmation you need to include in your regular practice. Most of the affirmations in this book have several variations, making it easy for you to choose the wording that most resonates with you.

Evolving your affirmations

After a couple of months of practicing your affirmations, you'll notice your feelings about them start to change.

Some affirmations will start to feel like you've repeated them so many times that they've lost their meaning. In these instances, I recommend switching to an affirmation that uses different phrasing to target the same belief. For example, you might switch from "I pay attention to my finances" to "I am strategic about my finances."

Other affirmations will become easy. You'll start to write them with confidence because, after months of work, you've internalized those positive beliefs. This means you're ready to start working on new ones. You'll find plenty of inspiration for those within these pages.

You may also decide that you need to work on beliefs I don't tackle in this book. In these instances, you'll want to create new affirmations using the structures found in this book. For example, if you want to build healthier eating habits, you might create the following affirmations:

- I enjoy healthy snacks.

- I control my relationship with food.

- I define my relationship with food.

You can use structures like these to build affirmations around any belief or habit you want to build.

With all of that in mind, it's time to dive into the affirmations themselves!

General
well-being

When I began my journey with affirmations, I wanted to make peace with myself. I wanted to foster a sense of appreciation for my mind and body. To live in, if not self-love, at least self-compassion instead of self-hatred.

I already knew the beliefs I wanted to tackle. I had lived with them all my life, repeated by the voice of my own treacherous mind: *I hate my body. I hate myself. I hate my life.*

Coming up with affirmations to challenge the beliefs was harder. Not because I didn't know the opposites; if you start with *I hate myself,* it's pretty clear that the other end of the spectrum is *I love myself.*

I wasn't ready for *I love myself,* though. Those words were such an obvious lie that my brain balked. Writing them down felt more than uncomfortable. It felt like pretending I was a whole other person. I could put the words on paper, but I couldn't make myself believe them.

So I met myself halfway. I created bridge statements: beliefs that felt like they *could* be true. *I care for myself* instead of *I love myself. I appreciate my body* instead of *I love my body. I'm glad to be alive* instead of *I love my life.*

These statements were uncomfortable, but there was a glimmer of possibility in them. A glimmer that grew as I wrote them for the tenth, fiftieth, hundredth time, until they became truths instead of merely things that *could* be true.

With these new beliefs in place, I was able to set my sights on more ambitious mental transformations. I changed my bridge statements to the positive statements they were always meant to help me reach: *I love myself, I love my body, I love my life.*

I expanded, too, adding affirmations of healing: *I choose healing, I let go of past hurts, I find peace within myself.* Affirmations of empowerment joined them: *I am strong, I choose my future, I build my own future.*

These affirmations, and the others found in this section, are designed to lay a strong mental foundation of confidence and self-love. They come first in the book for a couple of reasons. One, they were the beginning of my own journey to affirmations. Two, I believe many of us place too much of our self-worth in our creativity and the success of our careers. We are people before we are artists, before we are workers. If we want to heal, to become whole, we must acknowledge this. Starting with the affirmations in this chapter is a way to do exactly that.

You should use these affirmations if:

- You want to build a stronger sense of self-worth

- You want to build a sense of self-love

- You want to let go of toxic patterns, people, and beliefs

Affirmations for general well-being

I matter.

I am enough.

I am not too much.

I am powerful.

I am loved.

I am worthy.

I am resourceful.

I am resilient.

I believe in myself.

I love myself.

I enjoy my own company.

I deserve to take up space.

I deserve to be valued as a whole person.

I deserve love and compassion.

I am strong enough to ask for help.

I care for my health.

I show myself the same compassion I show my friends.

I am strong.

I am confident.

I am capable.

I am always growing, learning, and changing.

I am smart enough to learn the skills I need to thrive.

I make time for rest.

I deserve rest.

I seek out what nurtures me.

I choose compassion.

I choose forgiveness.

I choose healing.

I choose joy.

I choose love.

I choose rest.

I let go of anger and resentment.

I let go of past hurts.

I move toward healing and compassion.

I do the work required to heal.

I let go of things that no longer serve me.

I let go of limiting beliefs.

I let go of toxic habits.

I resist the urge to compare myself to others.

I resist the urge to see others as competition.

I let go of toxic relationships.

I attract healthy relationships.

I nurture healthy relationships.

I am worthy of unconditional love and support.

I am loved and supported.

I show myself love and support.

I surround myself with people who love and support me.

I do not need external validation.

I provide my own validation.

I am kind to myself.

I trust myself.

I love myself.

I choose peace.

I find peace within myself.

I find peace in solitude.

I create peace in my environment.

I foster my connection to nature.

I find peace in my connection to nature.

I seek growth.

I seek wisdom.

I seek joy.

I work to be the best version of myself every day.

I admit when I am wrong.

I am more than my mistakes.

I treat setbacks as learning opportunities.

I look for happiness within myself.

I embrace change.

I embrace opportunity.

I choose my future.

I define my future.

I believe in my future.

I build my own future.

Creativity

In my teens and early twenties, I had unwavering confidence in my writing. I believed I would be a full-time author by 30, with a whole slew of books out and a small but dedicated fan base.

I made good progress, too. I had a novella published by a small press. I created settings for a couple of TTRPGs. I successfully funded a book on Kickstarter.

Things changed in 2018. A series of unfortunate events in my personal life derailed my mental health. I spent months trying to restore my equilibrium. When I felt like I finally had it back in the summer of 2019, an unknown virus left me bedridden for eight days and struggling with constant fatigue for many months.

My second recovery was poorly timed, too, with the world going into lockdown right when I felt ready to go out again. Everything changed. I found myself suddenly carrying all of the rent and most of the other household expenses. Stress, isolation, and the increasingly horrifying state of the world destroyed what little focus I had regained.

2021 and 2022 were, in many ways, even worse for me than 2020. Life became a constant stream of stress and my writing slowed to a crawl. For the first time in my life, I began to wonder if I *could* build a successful writing career. I started to doubt my ability even to complete the next book. The one certainty that had carried me through the traumas of my teen years suddenly seemed shaky and unrealistic.

I wasn't prepared to give up, though. Storytelling is my deepest passion, the core of my being. As hard as it was (and sometimes still is) to imagine a successful future as an author, it was harder to imagine myself *not* writing. I had no other vision for my future. So I had to work my way back to believing in the vision I set out for myself at the tender age of eight years old: that someday I would tell stories for a living.

To achieve this, I created a new set of affirmations. Some to bolster my faith in my writing, others to set my intention for a renewed creative practice. I wrote them out night after night, using them to guide my mind back to a place of abundant creativity. I'm still finding ways to fit my creative process around my new obligations and health issues, but the ideas are flowing and I've once again become confident in my ability to succeed as an author. When I feel that confidence slipping, I return to the affirmations in this section to bolster it.

You should use the affirmations in this section if:

- You want to feel confident pursuing your art

- You want to feel confident applying for creative opportunities

- You want to create a more intentional creative process

Affirmations for creativity

I am creative.

I am an artist.

I am always developing my craft.

I invest in my art without guilt.

I invest in the best creative tools I can afford.

I spend time on my art without guilt.

My art is valuable.

My art is worth investing in.

I am a skilled artist.

My art is always becoming better.

I nurture my creativity with artistic play.

I bring a powerful, unique perspective to my art.

I prioritize the art that brings me joy.

I find joy in my art.

I challenge myself creatively so I can grow.

I enjoy creative challenges.

I see creative obstacles as opportunities to grow.

I deserve creative opportunities.

I seek out creative opportunities with confidence.

I make my own creative opportunities.

I see creative opportunities others do not.

I cultivate creativity in my everyday life.

I make space for creativity in my daily routine.

I cultivate creativity in my environment.

I find creative ways to improve every aspect of my life.

I find creative ideas everywhere.

My creativity is powerful.

My art is powerful.

My art is worthy.

I surround myself with people who nurture my creativity.

I distance myself from people who discourage my creativity.

I pursue creative knowledge at my own pace.

I see the value in my own art.

I resist the urge to compare myself to other artists.

I see other artists as my colleagues, not my competition.

I create my own inspiration.

I refuse to limit my own creativity.

I seek knowledge and mentorship from artists I admire.

I deserve artistic success.

I embrace artistic success.

I create my own artistic success.

Career

Like most writers, I also have another career to pay the bills. I write and edit articles about how to use WordPress, and I've been doing it for 10 years. Still, I struggle to accept the mantle of "expert". Every time I raise my rates, a little voice asks if I'm really worth so much. When a company approached me about full-time work in 2021, I was confused, wondering why they want to work with me—even though I have a decade's worth of articles to prove my skills and knowledge.

I also fear success, or more accurately, I fear something essential to creating my success: hiring people. The idea of finding people I want to work with is exhausting. The idea of letting someone else handle even the most mundane business tasks is nerve-wracking. The idea of someone relying on me for some or all of their income is even more terrifying.

In order to build the life I want, I must challenge the beliefs these fears are based on. I need to believe I am worthy of awards and capable of running workshops at even the most prestigious of institutions. I need to have faith in my ability to find trustworthy, reliable people who can help me expand my business. I need to believe in my ability to earn enough to pay those people.

I speak about these beliefs in the present tense because I'm still struggling with them. My confidence in my career seems to wax and wane with the moon. Some nights my career-related affirmations feel true, other nights they feel uncomfortable. On my worst nights, they feel like outright lies, things that will never be true no matter how hard I try to believe them.

Still, I have seen some progress. Affirmations like *I deserve career opportunities* and *I am confident in my professional skills* became things I believe rather than just things I write down sometimes. I'm more comfortable with the statement *I seek out career opportunities with confidence* than I was a year ago, a fact that becomes self-evident when I look at how many things I've submitted to in the past six months. With time, I'm confident I can build the confidence I need to take both of my businesses to the next level.

Most of the affirmations in this section are affirmations I'm either currently using or planning to use in the future. Others are based on common fears and internal struggles talked about in creative communities. I've also included a mix of affirmations that are specific to creative careers and more generalized affirmations that can apply to any career. I hope this mix of affirmations will help you find success in all of your professional endeavors, whether they're creative or not.

You should use the affirmations in this section if:

- You want to build confidence around applying to/interviewing for jobs

- You want to feel confident asking for promotions and career opportunities

- You want to stop caring about arbitrary measures of success set out by society and start focusing on *your* definition of success

- You want to stop caring about arbitrary measures of success set out by society and start focusing on *your* definition of success

Affirmations for career

I am confident in my professional skills.

I approach interviews with confidence and calm.

I approach promotions with confidence and calm.

I am smart enough to learn the career skills I need to thrive.

I deserve recognition for my art.

I deserve career opportunities.

I deserve to be paid for my art.

I sell my art with confidence.

I submit my art with confidence.

I belong on panels at conferences and conventions.

I will find my 1,000 true fans.

I seek out career opportunities with confidence.

I make my own career opportunities.

I see career opportunities others do not.

I define my own success.

I create my own success.

I attract success.

I embrace success.

Finance

As a kid, the main thing I knew about money was that my parents didn't have any. I knew it because of the awful apartment we lived in, the hand-me-down clothes that made up most of my wardrobe, the low quality of the food we ate. I felt it every time my parents couldn't afford the special pizza lunch at school or the books in the Scholastic flyers they handed out in class every month.

In those years, money was an aspiration. I wanted to earn enough of it to break the chains of poverty. I wanted to eat pizza whenever I desired it, buy every interesting book I found, and have a beautiful home filled with all of those books and cozy nooks to read them in. I built elaborate mental visions of my future as a middle-class author, someday moving to Scotland to live by the sea and pursue my passion for writing in solitude.

The role money played in my life has been many things since then. A reward, giving me something tangible to prove the value of my work. A temptress, pulling me toward impulsive purchases and outrageous parties. A tool, helping my family survive and making it possible to publish my books.

Most often, though, money has been an obstacle. The cost of traveling kept me from exploring the world. The cost of tuition prevented me from going to university. The cost of rent in my city has kept my family in the same one-bedroom apartment long past the point where we've outgrown it. The cost of living makes it impossible for me to focus full-time on the books I'm so passionate about writing. Nearly every time I've failed to manifest a dream or desire, it has been because I lacked the money to make it happen.

This led to the development of a whole host of negative emotions surrounding money. Anger at how much everything costs, despair at the way my paycheque disappears in minutes, shame that I can't find a way to make it work and live my dreams. I became overwhelmed by these emotions and the entire idea of money, and I gave up. I stopped paying attention to my finances beyond making sure I never went to the store unless I had money to pay for what I wanted. I didn't think about getting out of debt or saving money. I even ignored my taxes for a few years.

In some ways, it was easier. I wasn't making enough money to aggressively pay debts or save large amounts, and it *was* a relief to stop pressuring myself to do those things. But the debt didn't go away and the pile of tax paperwork kept on growing, leaving me with a looming sense of doom that filled my mind whenever I had a quiet moment. A sense of doom worsened by film, the industry my spouse worked in, virtually disappearing overnight when the pandemic hit.

This is probably where you expect me to say I turned to my journal, but affirmations weren't the first step to recovery in my relationship with money. The first step wasn't even one I took myself: it was the reappearance of the film industry. With my spouse earning a halfway decent wage, I had some financial room to breathe.

Sometimes you need to change your circumstances before you can change your mind. My money situation was one of these instances. If I had started money-related affirmations before my spouse returned to working in film, my mental voice would have met each word with bitter laughter. I had real, tangible proof of my financial failures and the dismal financial situations most folks found themselves in at the beginning of the pandemic. I needed real, tangible evidence of financial success, however small, to make finance-related affirmations feel like they *could* be true.

There comes a time, though, when your external circumstances can't improve any further until your internal ones do. I've reached this point in my financial life, where I have enough money to improve my life and the things holding me back are my lack of confidence and intention around how I approach money. So I've incorporated financial affirmations into my practice: *I control my spending, I am confident with money, I embrace wealth.*

Many of the affirmations in this section have become permanent fixtures in my mind, beliefs that inform how I operate in my everyday life. Others are beliefs I am still struggling with. All were designed to heal my relationship with money. I hope they'll help you heal your relationship with money too.

You should use the affirmations in this section if:

- You want to become comfortable managing money

- You want to become comfortable talking about money

Affirmations for finance

I pay attention to my finances.

I control my spending.

I approach financial management with confidence.

I am not ashamed of my financial situation.

I am not ashamed of my spending habits.

I am not ashamed to talk about money.

I am comfortable talking about money.

I am comfortable asking for help with money.

I can become better at controlling my money.

I can learn new financial management skills.

I am more than my financial situation.

My financial future is not defined by my financial past.

I let go of limiting beliefs around money.

I invest in myself.

I invest in my future.

I treat financial missteps as learning opportunities.

I embrace new financial tools.

I attract wealth.

I deserve wealth.

I embrace wealth.

Creating your own affirmations

Negative beliefs often permeate every aspect of our lives, and this workbook can't possibly tackle every negative belief you might have. This makes it essential to learn to create your own affirmations.

You can do this in four steps

Step one: list your negative beliefs

Set a timer for three minutes and list all of the negative things you believe about yourself during that time. Make sure to write down everything that comes to mind, no matter how small it seems; if you're thinking about it, there's a reason.

Step two: consider how these negative beliefs impact your life

Look at each negative belief and ask yourself some questions. What areas of your life are impacted by this belief? How often are they impacted? How strongly are they impacted? How would your life change if you believed something different?

You can write out your answers to these questions OR reflect on them mentally.

Step three: rank your negative beliefs in terms of how destructive they are

Rank the negative beliefs in terms of how much each one impacts your life. For example, a ten is something that has a major impact on your daily life, whereas a one is something that only occasionally impacts your life and/or doesn't interfere with your ability to function.

Once you've ranked them, circle the 2-3 beliefs causing the most harm to your everyday life. These are the beliefs you'll want to tackle with your affirmations.

Step four: write down an opposite belief to combat each negative belief

These opposite beliefs should use specific language to make sure they're effectively targeting your damaging beliefs. For example, if your damaging belief is "I hate myself", the opposite belief is "I love myself".

Here are a few more examples of opposite beliefs:

- "I deserve to be surrounded by love" is the opposite of "I don't deserve love"

- "I love my body" is the opposite of "I hate my body"

- "I am a great artist" is the opposite of "I am a terrible artist"

- "I deserve artistic recognition" is the opposite of "I'm not good enough to be a featured/highlighted/paid artist"

Note that these all use similar language to the negative belief. This makes it more difficult for your brain to twist the opposite belief to mean something else.

Write your own opposite beliefs down using a similar strategy.

Optional: create bridge statements

In some instances, you might find an opposite belief too uncomfortable to sit with, enough so that you start avoiding your affirmation practice altogether. When this happens, I suggest meeting your brain halfway with a bridge statement.

I discussed bridge statements at the beginning of this book, but here's a quick recap: a bridge statement is a neutral or mildly positive belief that challenges the entrenched negative one. You can often create a bridge statement by changing one word in the opposite belief. For example, if you can't bring yourself to think "I love myself", you might choose to challenge "I hate myself" with "I like myself."

This also works for some of the opposite beliefs I mentioned in step four:

- "I am a great artist" can be "I am a decent artist"

- "I love my body" can be "I like my body"

In other cases, however, you'll need to change the whole sentence to create a bridge statement. For example, "I deserve to be surrounded by love" might become "I deserve to be treated with compassion" or "I deserve to be treated with respect."

Since you've already written out your negative beliefs and opposite statements, finding your bridge statement should be pretty easy. All you need to do is look at what you've already written down and ask yourself what the neutral statement between them is. That neutral statement then becomes the bridge you use to get from being stuck in the negative belief to the opposite one.

Thought-stopping with affirmations

As you sit down to choose your first set of affirmations, remember that changing your mind through affirmations is a long-term process. Writing affirmations once might be an interesting exercise, but if you're going to experience deep, meaningful change, you need to build a consistent affirmation practice.

You can also increase the power of affirmations by using them outside of your regular affirmation practice with a technique called thought-stopping or, as I first heard it called on The REL Show, "thought babysitting."

The concept is simple: you pay attention to your self-talk and, when you have a negative thought about yourself, you challenge it with a bridge statement or an affirmation. Over time, you get used to thinking or saying the more positive thought, and it comes more naturally to you than the negative one.

I've seen recommendations for a couple of other ways to do this, too:

Investigative thought-stopping

In this method, when you have a negative thought you don't challenge it with an affirmation right away. Instead, you ask yourself: is this a fact or a feeling? If it's not a fact, what are the facts? Chances are, the facts are more neutral or even positive. They might even lead directly to your affirmations.

Here's an example of how this method might work:

You drop a glass, it shatters, and as you're cleaning up you catch yourself thinking "I break everything I touch." You pause to ask yourself if this is true. Do you really break everything, or are there things you've been able to keep, unbroken, for years?

Your brain answers with one object, then another. A set of glass candle holders, dishes you've had for years, art, and books that you've treated with great care. Pretty soon you're thinking "I rarely break things" or "I'm actually pretty good at keeping important items safe." Through investigating your negative belief, you've realized it's not true and arrived at a more positive conclusion about yourself.

Advantages of this method

The big benefit of this technique is that when you arrive at a positive thought by assessing the facts, it's often easier to believe. You came to it naturally, after all, rather than forcing the affirmation out right away.

Disadvantages of this method

The only real disadvantage of this method is that it takes longer than the basic thought-stopping technique. If you're in the middle of doing something important, you don't really have the time to stop and fully investigate every negative thought. This means that this technique is most useful when you're not in a hurry or trying to do something that requires focus.

Repetitive thought-stopping

This is more like the original method I mentioned, except that you use three affirmations for each negative thought. You can either repeat the same affirmation three times or use different affirmations that target specific aspects of a negative belief.

Here's an example of how this might work, using the same dropped glass scenario:

You're cleaning up the glass you dropped when you catch yourself thinking "I break everything I touch." Since you're still looking for small pieces of glass, you don't want to get distracted, so you quickly challenge the thought by repeating "I am good at keeping important items safe" three times.

Advantages of this method

This technique is great because you end up thinking the positive thought more times than you had the negative thought. This may make the positive thought become a fully-fledged belief more quickly.

Disadvantages of this method

Like the first method discussed in this section, the repetitive thought-stopping technique doesn't really investigate the negative belief or what might be true. This may make the affirmations feel like they're being forced or even like they're outright lies.

The true challenge of thought-stopping

Thought-stopping is easy to explain but difficult to implement, especially if you've lived with negative beliefs about yourself for a long time. You might not even notice them until you're half an hour deep into a spiral of negative self-talk. When you do start noticing them and trying to challenge them, your affirmations might feel false and the whole effort pointless.

In some cases, all you need to get over this is time and practice. You'll become aware of every negative thought as it's happening, and you'll find yourself naturally creating positive statements to challenge them with.

In other cases, however, you'll need more support to make this happen. I personally didn't have much luck with thought-stopping until I was diagnosed with ADHD and started on medication. My thoughts were so fast that I didn't realize the negative self-talk was happening until I had been at it for several minutes. Now, however, I can slow down enough to challenge negative beliefs as they come up throughout my day.

This leads me to my final point: if you're struggling with this or any of the other practices in this book, or you feel like there's even a slight chance you might need therapy and/or medication, please seek psychiatric assessment and therapeutic treatment. This book is meant as a supplement to professional treatment, not a replacement for it.

Further resources for healing

Content note: This section includes mentions of trauma, mental illness, self-harm, and suicide. Please take care when reading or skip ahead to the resource lists if you don't feel comfortable reading about these topics.

Our mental struggles come from many places: traumatic events, abusive parents and family members, bullying at school or work. Our society manufactures new struggles too, bombarding us with messages about our inadequacies in the hope of getting us to buy more. We've been programmed to hate ourselves since we were children, developing anxiety, depression, and eating disorders before we even hit puberty. We've internalized these disorders and made them part of our identities.

When you've lived with self-hatred and mental illness for most of your life, healing requires monumental effort. You need to find new ways of thinking. You need to build coping mechanisms and processing tools. You need to cut toxic people out of your life and start building a network of supportive, loving humans. Your entire life needs to change, and you need to make all of these changes in a consumerist society determined to make you feel inadequate.

If you want to complete the long, messy journey of healing, you'll need a lot more than this book to get you there. In the next few pages, you'll find books, podcasts, and YouTube channels/videos that have helped me in my own healing journey. I hope they'll help you as well.

I also want to encourage you to seek help beyond what you can find in a book or a podcast. If you live in a place where therapy is accessible, find a therapist or a group therapy program to be part of. If you can't find a way to access therapy, seek out support groups for people with similar struggles. Many support groups are at least partially online, allowing you to participate from wherever you are in the world.

If you feel like you can't wait for therapy or access to a support group, or if you're struggling with thoughts of self-harm or suicide, please call a mental health hotline for immediate help. I've included the phone numbers for mental health hotlines in Canada, the US, the UK, and Australia at the end of this section. Many other countries have this type of hotline as well. I don't have the space to list them all here—and if I tried, I would likely still miss some—but you can find them with a quick Google search.

For now, it is time for you to move on to the next steps of your journey.

I hope the resources listed here will guide you through them, all the way to wholeness.

Books

Legacy: Trauma, Story, and Indigenous Healing by Suzanne Methot

Turn Your Pain Into Art by Ariel Bloomer

The Successful Author Mindset by Joanna Penn

Braiding Sweetgrass by Robin Wall Kimmerer

The Science of Stuck by Britt Frank, LSCSW

Unwinding Anxiety by Judson Brewer

The Happiness Project by Gretchen Rubin

Blogs

Blurt

Natasha Tracy BiPolar Burble

The Mighty

Love and Life Toolbox

Wounded Times

YouTube channels and videos

Kati Morton

Ask Kati Anything with Kati Morton

The REL Show's Self Love and Happiness playlist

Therapy in a Nutshell

Podcasts

The Happiness Lab

The Self Work Podcast

Not Another Anxiety Podcast

Bad with Money with Gaby Dunn

Mental health hotlines

Canada general mental health hotline - 1-866-585-0445

Talk Suicide Canada - 1-833-456-4566

US - 988

UK Samaritans - 116123

UK Shout Crisis Text Line - Text "SHOUT" to 85258 or "YM" if you're under 18

Australia Lifeline - 13 11 14

Beyond Blue Australia - 1300 22 4636

151 Affirmations for Creative People: The Workbook

Want some more hands-on guidance for creating your affirmation practice? Check out 151 Affirmations for Creative People: The Workbook. This mini-workbook features questions designed to help you with every aspect of building your affirmation practice, from choosing your affirmations to creating new affirmations of your own.

This workbook is designed as a companion to the main *151 Affirmations for Creative People* book. You can buy it in paperback through Amazon or grab the PDF edition from https://ko-fi.com /diannagunn/shop.

Acknowledgments

This book wouldn't be possible without the support of friends, family, and colleagues over the past couple of years. I've done my best to thank everyone here. If you don't see your name, know that it doesn't mean I don't appreciate your help; it simply means that so many people have touched the making of this book, and my life during the making of this book, that I don't have space to list them all.

First and foremost I want to mention my best friend, Samantha Kennedy, whose offhanded comment about affirmations led me on the journey of developing an affirmation practice and later writing this book. Your friendship has been a rock that has held me steady through many tumultuous times in my life. Moreover, your dedication to bettering yourself and finding ways to thrive in today's chaotic world inspires me to do the same every day.

Next, I want to mention my spouse, Astrid Fairwinds, who has always supported my quest to become an author. I hope we have many decades of adventures still to come.

I also want to thank Robbie Murphy, a dear friend whose dedication to the hard work of healing has always inspired me. You've always been there for me, and that friendship has never been more appreciated than in the past three years. I hope I can always do the same for you.

Another chosen family member I want to thank is Felix. Your presence always brings joy into my life.

Most of my family is chosen, but there are also some incredible people in the family I was born to. Shane Gunn, Victoria Roth, Tanja Gunn, Talia Johnson: I am so glad to know I have your support in all of my endeavors.

And, of course, I have to give a shoutout to everyone who directly helped me bring this book into reality. Starting with Steven Savage, who helped me with both the cover art and the editing for this book. Jade Benjamin, my long-time friend, editor, and business partner, who convinced me that it was worth learning to format books so I could release this in paperback. Cait Gordon, whose encouragement kept me going when I thought this book, and everything else, was pointless.

Finally, I want to thank you, the person reading this book. Whether you've supported everything I've done or you didn't know I existed before you found this book, I'm grateful you chose to spend your time with my words. I hope they help you develop a healthy relationship with yourself.

About Author

Dianna Gunn is a freelance blogger, fantasy horror novelist, founder of the Weeknight Writers Group, and about a dozen other things. She has lived with depression and anxiety for as long as she can remember and spent most of her life struggling to heal from traumatic events in her youth. As she heals and grows, she hopes to share the tools and practices that have helped her with others struggling with mental illness.

You can find all of Dianna's nonfiction work at https://ko-fi.com /diannagunn/shop or check out her novels at https://authordian nagunn.com.

www.ingramcontent.com/pod-product-compliance
Lightning Source LLC
Chambersburg PA
CBHW070816050426
42452CB00011B/2066